T0016957

A true story from the Bible

ESTHER
and the very
BRAVE
PLAN

·WRITTEN BY·
Tim Thornborough

·ILLUSTRATED BY·
Jennifer Davison

We all make plans.
We make a plan to see friends.
We make a plan to go on a journey.
We make a plan to go swimming or have a picnic.

This is a true story from the Bible about some
horrible men who made a horrible plan to get rid of
God's people. But it's also a story about how God had
a secret plan to rescue his people.

As you read this story, try to spot how God
is secretly at work to make his plan work,
and the other plans fail.

Esther and the Very Brave Plan © The Good Book Company, 2021. Reprinted 2022 (twice), 2024.
Words by Tim Thornborough. Illustrations by Jennifer Davison. Design and art direction by André Parker.
thegoodbook.com • thegoodbook.co.uk • thegoodbook.com.au • thegoodbook.co.nz • thegoodbook.co.in
ISBN: 9781784986209 | JOB-007705 | Printed in India

In the land of Persia, in the great, great city of Susa, there lived a great and powerful king.

The king was rich and proud.

But the king had a problem.

To go with his beautiful gold and his beautiful palaces, the king wanted a beautiful queen.

So the proud king made a proud plan.

He ordered the most beautiful women in Persia to come to his palace so he could choose one of them to be his new queen.

Esther lived with her cousin Mordecai in the great, great city of Susa.

They were God's people, and they lived in the land of Persia along with many others who loved and served the one true God.

Now God had made Esther a very beautiful woman. So when the king saw her, he chose her to be queen. The proud king's proud plan had worked.

But the king wasn't the only one with a plan. God had a plan too, and he was secretly working, working, working to make it happen.

One day Mordecai heard two wicked men making a wicked plan to get rid of the king.

Mordecai went and told the king, and the wicked men with the wicked plan were stopped. The king was saved!

What Mordecai did was written in a special book.

This was all part of God's secret plan and God was secretly working, working, working to make it happen.

Now Haman was the king's special helper.

Haman HATED God's people.

But he hated Mordecai most of all.

"I will get rid of Mordecai," he said. "And I will get rid of ALL of God's people as well!"

So horrible Haman made a horrible plan.

Haman said to the king,

"There are people in your kingdom who love and serve the one true God and who do not obey you. You should make a law that they should all be killed."

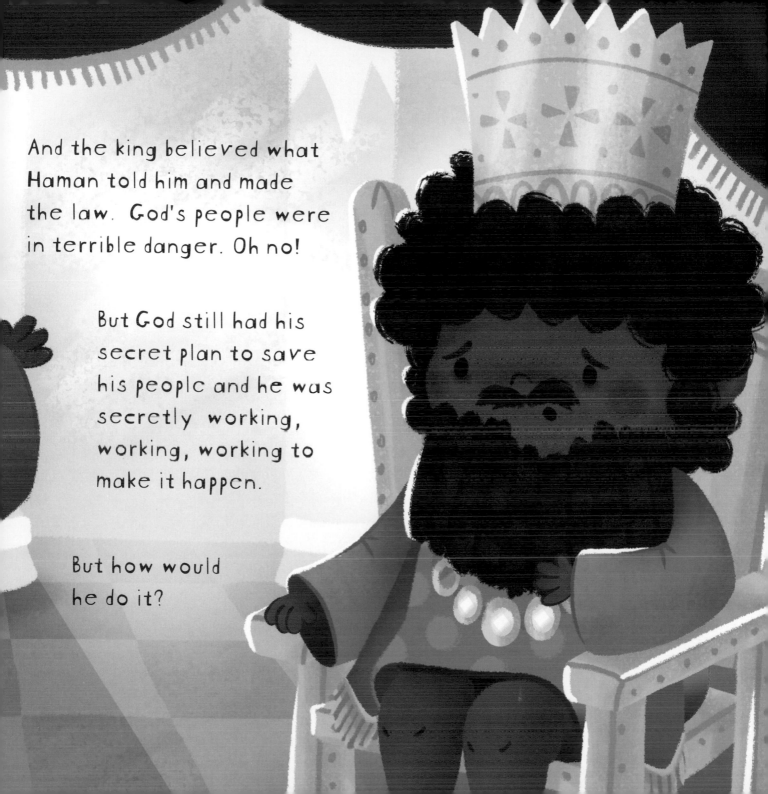

And the king believed what Haman told him and made the law. God's people were in terrible danger. Oh no!

But God still had his secret plan to save his people and he was secretly working, working, working to make it happen.

But how would he do it?

Mordecai heard about the horrible plan, and sent a message to Esther.

"We are all in terrible danger.

Maybe this is the reason you are queen — for such a time as this."

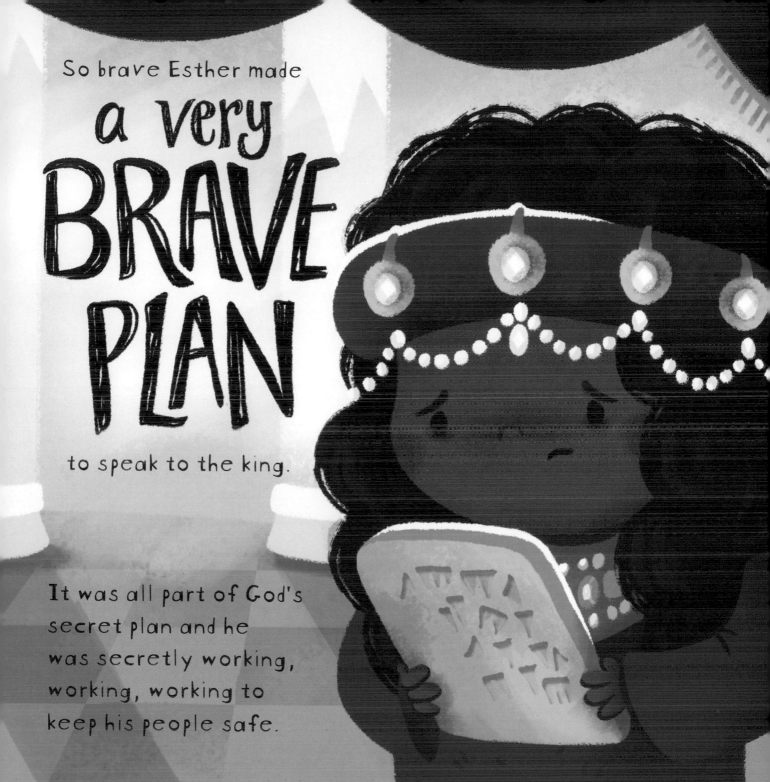

So brave Esther made

a very BRAVE PLAN

to speak to the king.

It was all part of God's secret plan and he was secretly working, working, working to keep his people safe.

Now in the land of Persia, no one could just walk up and talk to the king — not even the queen!

But brave Esther put on her royal robes, and walked — trembling — in to see him.

She knew it was a very dangerous thing to do.

But the king looked at her and smiled.

So Esther invited the king and Haman to come to a special dinner the next day.

That night the king could not sleep, and he asked for his special book to be read to him.

His servant told the story of how Mordecai had saved him from the wicked men with the wicked plan.

So the king ordered that Mordecai should be led through the streets on his royal horse, and that everyone should bow down to him.

And he told Haman to lead the horse!

It was all part of God's secret plan and he was secretly working, working, working to save his people.

At the banquet with Queen Esther that night, the king and Haman had a wonderful time.

The king said to Esther, "Ask me anything, and I will give it to you".

Esther said, "Someone has ordered that I and all my people should be killed — please save us".

The king was angry: "Who did this?"
Esther said: "It's Haman!"

Haman was taken away. And Mordecai was made the king's special helper. God's people were saved. And they had a huge party to celebrate.

This was God's secret plan. He had been secretly working, working, working to rescue his people.

GOD'S PLANS ALWAYS come true -

even when we can't see how — and even when things seem to be going wrong.

God is always working, working, working to rescue his people so that they can celebrate with him for ever.